twelve THE KING

*Dedicated to
all who believe that
humanity is not the
only important element
on the planet earth.*

twelve THE KING, Michael Blake, ISBN 978-0-9819747-8-1, ©2009 Perceval Press, Perceval Press, 1223 Wilshire Blvd., Suite F, Santa Monica, CA 90403, www.percevalpress.com
Editor: Viggo Mortensen, Design: Michele Perez, Copy Editor: Sherri Schottlaender, Printed in Spain at Gráficas Jomagar S.L., Originally published in hardcover 2009

twelve THE KING

MICHAEL BLAKE

Perceval Press

TWELVE THE KING *a memorial written by Michael Blake*

It happened when I was eighteen, in the parking lot of a community college. A few miles off was a long, tall ridge. The sun was dropping, its yellowing light overwhelming a gigantic cloud with other visible air cutting in strings across it. The dying sun was shooting out glowing golden waves. The ridge appeared to be changing wildly, with only one item, near the far edge, showcased: It was a beautiful tree that looked as if it had been painted on. Everything was suddenly alien, and for the first time in my life I was struck that the being much of humanity describes as God was real.

When I was a kid, random attendance at Bible studies and hearing preachers preaching had only delivered boredom, but this was different. It was as if the life of earth and sky was daring me to explain how life had come to be. I couldn't—but I knew that it hadn't come from us. It had come from something unknown.

After that experience, I have never attended church. Preachers who speak to God, priests who listen to God, and prayers for consideration are not convincing—even the word "God" feels unconvincing. What Indians call "the Mystery" is the only reference to a higher power that I have ever found to be suitable. In the more than forty years that have passed since that enlightening view of the ridge, I have experienced a few more appearances of proof in the form of spiritual visions, psychic moments, and undefinable events.

And nearly twenty years ago I encountered an animal whose being was saturated with evidence that the Mystery's spirit was on earth.

It was Twelve.

LEFT:
Twelve and Samantha playing, 1992

While I had previously visited Reno and Las Vegas, after *Dances with Wolves* emerged as a film in 1990, I saw large portions of the rest of Nevada for the first time.

At the time everyone in Hollywood was knocking at my door with money in hand. One eminent producer tied to Universal Studios researched my life and discovered that I had an affinity for horses. He had also apparently found a magazine article about a law enforcement officer's investigation of a crime involving wild horses. He asked me if I could write a screenplay, and I said, "Sure."

A day or two later we walked into the studio president's office and sat down. The producer explained the story verbally in a paragraph or two and told the executive that I would need half a million dollars to write it. Without hesitation, the executive said, "Okay."

The meeting didn't even last five minutes.

Because I knew nothing about wild horses or the places they roamed, it was necessary to make some visits, the first one to the unique city of Reno. It was there that an elderly woman who came to be known as Wild Horse Annie saved the state's free horses from incessant killing. One day in 1950 she was driving down a street behind a huge truck trailer literally stuffed with horses. Waterfalls of blood were streaming out of the rear of the truck, so she followed it. Several animals inside had died because they were unable to move; those who had survived were being hauled to slaughter. Wild Horse Annie couldn't forget the horrible sights she had seen, and so she began a long-term fight, supported by unprecedented numbers of people, to protect wild horses. Federal legislation for protecting these animals—the Wild Horse and Burro Act—went into effect in 1971 and was still in place when I arrived in Reno to do research late in 1991.

Because I was known for writing *Dances with Wolves*, a book and movie that had worldwide impact, it was easy to arrange meetings with locals who were involved with wild horses. Several meetings were held in a large and beautiful hotel atop a gigantic casino. The suite where we met had a spectacular 180-degree bank of windows; these were not spectacular in their construction but rather because they enabled a spectacular view outside. Looking east into Nevada from a ten-story height, one had a perfect view of the small green city and the river that ran through its midst. But what happened after the city ended was mind-boggling: nothing could be seen but the planet itself with its hills, valleys, mountains, and sky. The seemingly endless view was like a look at Earth before life had appeared. It was actually an eerie sensation, because I'd never seen anything quite like it before. The ancient planet was only an eyeshot from civilization.

Several visitors came to the hotel room to talk with me. One was particularly memorable: a tough, fiftyish woman dressed in what I assumed were her "fancy" clothes. We spoke at length. It was clear that

TOP:
Twelve in Palomino Valley, 1991

BELOW:
Wild horses in confinement, BLM facility; Twelve at far right leading a group of wild horses

she had actively supported the cause of wild horses for years and that she was as deeply involved in the issue as ever, but when we discussed the federal agency in charge—the Bureau of Land Management, the BLM—I detected a faint yet distinctive sense of confusion. She worked routinely with the BLM and spoke of the feds in good terms. At the same time I saw changes in her expression, odd side comments, and body language that indicated the federal association had infected her brain with discomfort.

In the months to come we would convene and attend meetings together occasionally. Eventually we would go separate ways when I publicly expressed total opposition to the incompetence and corruption of the BLM. There was no fighting in our break, and I will always be grateful to her for taking me to Nevada's huge wild horse facility for the first time and introducing me to a man who would effect a monumental change in my life.

The place is called Palomino Valley. It is situated forty or fifty miles north of Reno and has only been seen by a tiny fraction of one percent of the American public. The drive up was special. After a few miles the signs of human creation all but vanished. An occasional house and fence appeared; we'd pass an abandoned gasoline station or a still-functioning, poorly built store selling food and drink. Traffic on the road was rare. What dominated one's vision was the approach to Nevada's incredibly sparse northeast desert. Treeless hills began to rise higher. Open plains dominated views to the horizon.

What seemed like a journey across a different planet was suddenly interrupted by the sight of a small valley area nestled between a long, running pair of oddly shaped hills. It was filled with the evidence of human workmanship in the form of gigantic corrals bigger than football fields, dirt parking lots, office trailers, trucks, lodges, horse haulers, storage, treatment barns, and tack lockers. About twenty men and women in cowboy hats were walking to and fro, engaged in various activities.

We parked and walked into the Bureau of Land Management headquarters, located in a trailer. Word was sent out to the director of the horse and burro camp that Michael Blake had arrived to meet him, and in minutes he appeared. Probably in his late fifties, the director was a life-long cowboy, well over six feet tall and with facial features that looked like those of an aging Western actor. From the moment we shook hands, it was clear to me that he was an honest and caring person.

That afternoon he led me on a tour. I saw the animals gathered in gigantic pens as the director explained the complex rail paths and endless gates that served as multiple systems for controlling the captives. While we walked, he described what the animals experienced after their capture: all males were castrated and separated from females and their young. Many had such hard hooves that it took a month or more before trimming them was possible. Wholesome hay and fresh water were constantly available, and adoptions were pursued rigorously.

Altogether the captives numbered at least in the high hundreds. All the animals I could see

after a few miles the signs of human creation all but vanished appeared to be healthy and reasonably content, a first impression that I later learned was deceptive. From my first view of what had been constructed in Palomino Valley, I found it impossible to think of a term other than these truthful words that refused to leave my head: It was a concentration camp. Every horse had been captured. Many had died during brutal roundups and the congested transports that could barely be endured. Families had been split forever. Each animal had to follow the orders of its captors. Freedom no longer existed.

The cowboy who headed the concentration camp obviously worked diligently to follow all the procedures for which he was responsible, but like the woman who had brought me to this place, his smiles were often tainted with a distinctive but indefinable melancholy.

After we'd spent a few hours together, the director invited me to make visits into the field to get a better understanding of why the BLM operation was necessary. On one trip we traveled many miles from Reno to arrive at a place where scores of wild horses were trying to consume the only water available to them, water they had to travel most of a day to reach. It was a pitiful sight—so many animals surrounding filthy ponds only inches deep. Removing them from such awful conditions seemed to be the only humane thing to do.

On another trip a few days later we visited a capture site. There, the freshly caught animals were having their age determined and their health status diagnosed through individual halts in squeeze pens before their ultimate transport to the concentration camp at Palomino. The man conducting the exams was the head of BLM captures; though not a working member of the federal agency, he and his men were frequently hired to bring in the horses. He and the people on his team were long-time Nevada residents who had exclusive knowledge about how to capture, examine, and transport wild horses.

Initially I had an altogether good feeling about the federal approach to this situation, a good feeling inspired by meeting the concerned director, touring Palomino, and visiting various sites in the field. At first I could easily support the government's action on this issue. It took relatively little time, however, for the connection and my goodwill to dissolve. All that I had seen was nothing more than fool's gold.

While an overpopulation of wild horses had seemed to be the main cause of the difficulty in finding water and food for them throughout the state, that turned out not to be the case: time after time these shortages were the result of premeditated blockage of access. Ranchers would fence off streams, and the BLM would respond positively to requests for removal when those who ran cows complained that wild horses were robbing their herds of vegetation.

It also took very little time to discover that the man responsible for the captures—as well as most of the men who worked for him—were criminals. The leader himself, even as he worked for the government, had been indicted by a grand jury for capturing and selling wild horses without approval.

many had died during brutal roundups and the congested transports that could barely be endured

Despite this, the government continued to hire and pay him and his gang.

These discoveries would prove to be superficial when compared to the depth of deceit, corruption, and criminality I uncovered. As is the case with mountain lions, wolves, and buffalo, there is an effort to rid America of wild horses. These creatures have never instigated conflict, but since the landing of the Pilgrims, animals and Indians' way of life in North America have been destroyed because they have been in the way. Although their numbers have been reduced from millions to perhaps thirty thousand, wild horses were still considered to be in the way.

None of this was clear to me on that first trip to Reno. In those first days I never saw anything that appeared to be brutal treatment, and the wild horses didn't look much different from the domestic animals I had ridden, groomed, and befriended since boyhood. Horses, regardless of the affection they inspire, are animals that are, in a most basic sense, useful to people, and that is how they are generally appraised.

I delayed returning to Los Angeles when the director at Palomino told me about an upcoming event that he believed would provide me with telling knowledge: the public was invited to a day-long affair at the concentration camp where adoptions would be pursued; there would also be lectures, tours, and exhibitions of the wild horses. He told me that observing the proceedings would be informative.

So, on the last day of my first visit, I returned to Palomino, again arriving at noon. The parking lot held perhaps thirty cars and trucks. Although fewer than a hundred people had come, the director and his wife, his staff, and their families actively engaged with those who had arrived, and they stayed busy preparing the exhibitions that would come after lunch. Despite the low attendance, being able to meet and talk to a perhaps uncertain public was an exciting opportunity for the federal employees to show that the work they were doing was positive.

After a long lunch period during which many of the attendees left, staff members set up bales of hay to be used as seats around a small circular training pen. Most of those who had adopted horses had already departed with their selected animals, leaving only about thirty people to view the remaining presentations; these included elderly couples as well as middle-aged and young people. A few children sat still for a few minutes before sprinting back and forth to ice cream and soda trucks parked around the pen.

Ignoring the relatively puny size of his audience, the dedicated concentration camp director began a modestly delivered but extremely knowledgeable lecture on the nature of horses in general, and wild horses specifically. The address was filled with telling details delivered casually, and the small group of listeners remained focused. It was obvious from the fifteen-minute introduction that the director was seeking to convince whoever he could that adopting, training, and living with a wild horse would be a pleasant experience.

BELOW:
Twelve in Palomino Valley, 1991

After concluding his talk by saying that wild horses' lack of experience with humans actually provided an advantage in training, the director stepped up onto the rails of the pen. A fenced pathway connected the pen with the outer reaches of the camp, and he called out to a pair of staffers sitting atop a gate several dozen yards away: "Let's send him in."

The two young workers, who held long sticks topped with flags, leaped down behind the gate, swung it open, and a few moments later succeeded in driving a young, disoriented gelding through the gate and down the path into the pen. Another staffer shut the pen gate behind him. Skittishly, the horse moved around the pen, wondering what was going to happen to him. The director held out a hand and the jumpy gelding came over to him, stretched out his nose, and then darted away fearfully. With a little chuckle the director told his viewers what we already knew, that this horse had never been ridden. Then he added something that seemed inconceivable: in less than half an hour one of the visitors would be able to ride the frantic mustang around the pen.

Taking a halter in hand and pushing his broad-brimmed cowboy hat high on his forehead, the director climbed over the fence and dropped into the pen. The horse watched his every move with intense anticipation. As the young gelding made his first panicked turns, the director cut him off again and again, and as the seconds passed the horse must have realized that retreat was impossible. The next time the director cut him off, the gelding, shivering with anticipation, stood in place. Without hesitation, the director placed a palm against the horse's neck and gave him a few slow strokes. The gelding's nervousness lessened, and the director strapped the halter around his head and began to lead the horse around the pen. If the gelding halted in fear, the director would stand still too. With subtle movement the man would start forward again, and every time the animal would follow.

What happened next can perhaps be compared to viewing a film so fantastic that the details have to be rewatched to be recalled. After a bridle and saddle were put on the gelding, the director mounted him. Despite the horse's confusion about the sudden weight on his back, the director used gentle body movements, low vocalizing, and soft hand movements in beautiful unity—and the gelding began to move. Within five minutes and without one miscue, they were jogging around the pen; they then stopped, turned, and jogged the other way. The gelding didn't know how to hold his head or move his feet or understand why he had to stop, but he did everything he was asked. Finally the director dismounted, led the gelding up to the fence, and asked the people sitting on the hay bales if anyone wanted to ride.

Without speaking, a middle-aged woman stood up and climbed over the fence. A few seconds later, she was sitting on the gelding as he jogged around the pen with the director holding the lead line to the halter. The woman stopped the horse, gave him a pat, and dismounted. The director applauded

TOP:
Twelve in Palomino Valley, 1991

BOTTOM:
Twelve in Arizona, 1996

her and the spectators sitting outside the pen clapped for them both. From the time the wild horse who had never been ridden appeared in the pen to the time the volunteer rider's feet touched the ground, no more than twenty minutes had passed.

As the gelding left the pen, a wave of silence splashed over the small group of people who had watched the amazing demonstration. They neither spoke nor stood up. No one knew what to do next. The moment was perfect for the director's next move. He stepped onto the lowest bar of the pen's fence and looked over at his audience. The congenial smile that he often wore became broader.

"Would anyone like to see a *real* wild horse?"

Most people didn't answer because they were unsure exactly what the director meant, but several folks responded with enthusiastic calls of "yes."

The director turned and once again called down to the staffers at the gate: "Send him in." What happened next was as intriguing and dramatic as a perfectly formed film, but it hadn't been imagined and constructed—it was real life.

The gate was some distance away, and sight lines were hampered by the blur of fronting fence rails. Only bits and pieces of movement along the pathways could be seen as we waited for the next arrival.

Suddenly, there was black at the gate. Among those watching, there was instantaneous surprise that seemed to erase all sound. I was struck by the feeling that what was coming through that gate had never been seen before—and I believe that the others in attendance felt the same way.

When the black horse came into full view, everyone eyed his approach; it was as if we had all been tranquilized. He was floating down the pathway, his feet touching the ground as if it were a thick cloud. He was moving with nothing but caution, dropping his nose now and then as he continued forward, without a trace of the panic usually seen in recently captured wild horses. Once or twice he stopped briefly to look over the fence lines on either side of him, but there was still no panic. His ears were constantly pointed in the direction he was looking. His deep black eyes were filled with a look of determined concern, but no fear.

He came into the pen—it seemed almost as if he levitated in—and for a minute everyone just stared at him. Even the restless children watched him. He was something from another time or place. To me, it was as if he had just stepped off a Spanish warship from hundreds of years ago.

He was of medium height, and the bones and flesh of his body were perfection. Except for an inch of white around the base of the ankle on his left rear leg, he was entirely black. Even his well-sculpted face was devoid of any other color. His long, thick mane had grown to his shoulder; his black tail, lush but not encumbering, fell short of the earth by no more than an inch. He was more than beautiful: he was entrancing.

he was floating down the pathway, his feet touching the ground as if it were a thick cloud

Branded in white on the left side of his buttocks were the numbers "1202."

The gate closed behind him but he gave it no attention. He was already moving from one position to another, analyzing his trap. The horse never focused on anyone who was watching, and he also didn't look at vehicles or buildings or respond to voices. He stared briefly at horses penned in the distance, but it was landscape, landscape stretching to the faraway horizon that drew his focus. Until his capture on March 12, 1990, he had been doing the same thing for more than twenty years: working as a guardian. He was a herd stallion, and even though he had been castrated, he would be one for the rest of his life.

The director flashed another smile and asked: "Would anyone like to go in and touch him?"

Before anyone else could respond, a tall, middle-aged man's arm shot up and he started for the pen's fence. The director started to give him some hints about how to proceed, but before he could finish the man started over the fence. The black stallion gave the man a darting glance from the corner of his eye then never looked at him again. He continued to survey the land as the volunteer slowly but steadily closed in on him. When he was close enough, the man lifted a hand. With the fingers spread, he pushed it forward, toward the stallion's neck.

What happened next took place so quickly and was so stunning that no two descriptions from those who viewed it would be the same. At the moment the man's fingers started toward his neck, the stallion vanished. There was no banging against the fence bars, no desperate whinnies, no kicking, hardly any sound. He was gone, like magic. The man tried two or three more times, and though his approaches varied, the results were the same: because of the horse's seemingly impossible moves—quicker than the blink of an eye—the man was never able to make contact.

Three more people, two of them women, tried to touch the horse, but none succeeded. As each new attempt was made with increasing speed, the stallion merely increased his own. The last attempt was made by a woman who smiled at those watching and threw up her hands in defeat as she gave up, invoking consolation laughter from the audience.

The director called for the gate to be opened, and the black horse left in the same manner he had arrived, floating back down the pathway. As the gate in the distance opened, he turned and disappeared. The event was over.

On the drive back to Reno that afternoon, I found that it wasn't possible to stop thinking about the black herd stallion. Staring out the long windows in the hotel room that night, I couldn't stop reflecting on what I had seen that afternoon. These words got onto paper quickly.

BELOW:
Twelve's first public appearance, Nevada, 1991

he was gone, like magic . . . quicker than the blink of an eye

Horse Number 1202

Twenty years on the open range
Twenty years of running
Twenty years a stallion

Answering to no one

Now he is horse number 1202
Prowling a circular pen of steel
Moving lightly over the soft earth
Sniffing
Waiting
And moving again

Unbowed

He is forced to acknowledge
The man and woman
Inside the pen
Avoiding them perfectly
As he travels
Around and around

He looks through
The people crowded in the stands
The children pushing toy trucks on the packed
ground
The square, white lunch truck standing in the
back

He cares nothing for the flying flags
Or the video cameras
Or questions from the audience

Or for what's missing
From between his legs

It is the horizon

That is what holds his attention
The meeting place of sky and earth
Is the only destiny

He has ever known

A gate opens
And he swings his magnificent, black body
Around to face it
Now he treads carefully out
Dancing on air
His wise head
Low for danger
His flowing tail arched
His monstrous neck
Rippling with power

In city traffic
I remember his eyes
So dark and wet
So full of God

BELOW:
Twelve's last day in Nevada, 1991

13

The next morning I returned to Los Angeles.

Only days after I had returned to L.A., I came back to Reno. Further research for the screenplay was necessary, as were more meetings with knowledgeable area residents, but none of those reasons were why I really wanted to return. It was really because of him. While I had multitudes of feelings—including curiosity and concern—all that really mattered was my overwhelming desire to lay eyes on that horse again.

I dumped my duffel in a hotel room and immediately turned the car straight north to the concentration camp. Fortunately it was early afternoon, and the director was on site. He seemed pleasantly shocked to see me again, and after a few minutes of catching up, I asked about the small wild stallion. Without the hint of a question, he suggested that we go take a look.

The horse was alone in a long and wide high-fenced pen; there was a manger filled with hay hanging off one of the sides. He glanced in our direction but made no other acknowledgment of our presence. It was easy to see that he was hanging in an indefinable center of gravity: his head was not down, but it wasn't up, either. He stood in stillness, occasionally making a slow turn of his eyes in reaction to some movement or sound. He had been removed from the natural environment he knew, separated from his community and his mates and the scores of children he had raised. Here there was nothing but bare dusty ground, food and water that appeared from nowhere, and cell bars. He was too superior to attack or collapse. All he could do was wait.

As we watched the stallion we had a casual conversation. The director said that the captive in the pen was a horse the likes of which he had never encountered. He explained that during the day the captured animals were turned out into the football-field sized corrals spread around the concentration camp. He stopped speaking for a moment, and there was silence as he stared over at the herd stallion. Then he began to speak in a strange low tone that sounded like confession.

He told me that when the group of sixty to seventy recently castrated males to which the herd stallion belonged was let outside, the small black horse would walk firmly but without concern to the center of the huge space and come to a stop—and he would maintain his stance for the entire day. The scores of other horses would bite and kick each other, gallop around in circles, divide themselves into groups, and generally move about in moderate frustration. He said he had seen the black horse turn to look in different directions, but he had never seen him leave the center of the space.

There seemed to be an invisible barrier surrounding him, and none of the other horses, whether alone or in gangs, ever sniffed or touched or whinnied at him. They stayed outside his realm by a dozen or more feet. The director recalled that on one occasion the entire population came together and circled their king in a massive surround that lasted several minutes.

14

the entire population came together and circled their king

When the horses were moved into smaller pens, the one marked 1202 would start first for the exit. All the others would wait until he had moved several yards, then they would come together, fall in behind, and follow him.

When the director finished his story, he slipped off his white cowboy hat and dragged the palm of his hand down the front of his face.

"What do you make of that?" I asked.

He sighed, then looked at me with an uncertain smile.

"I don't know."

"What are those numbers on his flank for?"

"Slaughterhouses aren't allowed to take horses with numbers on their rears."

Looking at the distinctive numbers glowing in pure white on his black coat, I felt a sense of urgency rather than security.

"Well . . . what's going to happen to him?"

He settled the hat back on his skull and glanced once more over the fence he was leaning against. He said that the animal had been declared unadoptable, mainly because of his advanced age, so he couldn't give a concrete answer as to what his future would be. It soon became clear that, best case, the horse we were looking at would likely spend the rest of his life in the pen where he stood now.

We talked a while longer, hitting topics like the movie business, his past as a cattle rancher, and big cities, but we continually returned to the uniqueness of the animal we were watching.

The sun had started down and our talk was ending. I couldn't wait any longer—I had to say out loud what was now embedded in my brain. I looked the director straight in the eyes.

"You know what? . . . If I could adopt him, I would."

For a second he was surprised, then he nodded.

"I'd love it if you could have him." A smile spread across his face.

The next day I arrived at the office, signed the adoption papers, and passed over a check for one hundred and twenty dollars.

I was able to stay a couple more days, and much of that time was spent at the pen of my newly adopted wild horse. Just being in his presence was wonderful. One thing had to be done, however: he had to be haltered so that he could be given health care when necessary. Trying to get a halter around his head seemed impossible. It could be done, but it often took a half hour or more to even get a line around his neck.

The director told me that a much stronger effort would have to be made, and halter in hand, he went into the pen. Every time the stallion moved, the director would aggressively cut him off with quick

TOP:
The director eyeing Twelve, Nevada, 1991

BOTTOM:
Michael and Twelve, Nevada, 1991

15

feet and a sharp growl. In no time the stallion gave up, and the halter was soon on his head.

I then successfully used the same technique, but even though it was necessary, I didn't like it. I dreamed of a deeper connection between us, one that could only be made without a hint of domination.

In the years to come there would be rare times—for example, when he required medical treatment or physical examinations—when I had no choice but to be forceful with him. Even so, I avoided discipline whenever possible, because when I first saw this horse I was struck by feelings that I would only fully understand later: I worshipped him.

Over the next several weeks I made many trips between Los Angeles and Reno. Arrangements had to be made for his arrival in L.A., and using my writing about wild horses for Hollywood as an excuse, I was able to satisfy my largely inexplicable need to be near him.

Each visit I made to the concentration camp increased the pressure to remove him. Information I received from pro–wild horse activists in the area as well as my observation of the BLM workers led to inevitable conclusions: mainly, that the government's program for managing wild horses was a façade. Although I hadn't initially seen it, deceit, deception, and criminal activity infused all of the BLM's procedures.

The more time I spent with the director, the more clear it became that he had felt trapped in a vise for many years. He never spoke about it directly, but in a short time it was clear that his legitimate desire to provide for the captive horses was constantly being battered by shifting orders from his superiors, orders that were geared not toward preservation but toward eventual extermination.

Despite the differences in our stances, we remained personally engaged. In retrospect, perhaps the adoption of a one-of-a-kind horse by an internationally known writer provided a wisp of honesty to the incessant hypocrisy.

On my first return visit after the adoption, the director asked if I had chosen a name.

"Oh yeah," I replied. "Twelve."

"Oh, you took it from the number?"

"Nope. I just figured that if he was given a rating between one and ten, he'd have to be a twelve . . . at least."

The director responded with a chuckle. "You got that right."

My focus remained on being at the concentration camp and standing next to Twelve. I hoped that the hours spent together would be effective in forming a bond between us. Although the bond I imagined never did form, its nonexistence was never a disappointment—everything Twelve did while we were together lifted my life spirit to levels I had never experienced.

After the halter was on him, we would walk for hours. There were no uproars, outbursts, panics,

human existence had never been a factor in the way he conducted his life or runaways, not even slight ones. Twelve remained exactly the same as he was when I first saw him. He never looked at me, and his eyes never stopped evaluating his surroundings, especially those in the distance. Who I might be, where we were going, what might be done next didn't matter to Twelve. Human existence had never been a factor in the way he conducted his life, and it never would be. Although I would never be able to discern his thoughts, likes, dislikes, wishes, or hopes, they constantly swirled around me like some form of heavenly mist.

One thing became clear from the beginning and overarched all other considerations: I was with a creature whose connection with the earth upon which he walked was at a degree of perfection. Even life and death were not an issue. The proper conduct of every moment of existence was his sole reason for being.

At one point I met a professional photographer from New York City. She had been photographing wild horses for nearly a month, including despicable captures, haulings, and violent treatment, but when she met Twelve she became entranced, and she shot hundreds of photographs of him. Not one of the pictures indicates that he had any concern about the man holding the line to his halter, nor was he interested in the movement of vehicles or people. In every shot he is steady and calm, just as he was when he entered the pen the first time I saw him or as he stood statuesque in holding corrals from sunup to sundown.

Whenever I placed a hand across his back or covered his neck or hugged his head, he remained perfectly calm; there was no resistance. Perhaps the touching was reassuring. He also might have lost any feeling for asserting himself because the only life he knew had been taken from him. All that was certain was that while he might look at a camera, he would never look directly at the person holding his lead. And this never changed for nearly fifteen years: touching any part of his body was like pushing a finger against concrete, but his spirit could never be altered.

The closer I came to getting him out of prison, the slower time seemed to move, and it grew harder and harder to wait. Coordinating his removal from Nevada to Los Angeles was a complicated process, turtle-like in speed. My frustration reached a peak during my last visit to the concentration camp, but then the director brought a new proposition forward. He had given much thought to Twelve's future and was apprehensive that living completely alone might have a debilitating effect on him. Perhaps I should consider adopting another animal to live with him . . .

I asked if he had any ideas for a companion.

"Yeah, I do," he replied, smiling, and we walked to another pen holding a beautiful young mare who had been captured four years earlier at the age of three. She had come from Nevada's Black Rock Desert, an enormous region in the state's northeast corner that could be mistaken for another planet. Since her capture, the horse they called Samantha had failed to find a home. At first she had been

ABOVE:
*The director works to load
Samantha, Nevada, 1991*

17

transferred to a prison where qualified convicts were given opportunities to train wild horses, including Samantha. For unknown reasons she had been sent back to Palomino. Then she had traveled to Las Vegas to become a mascot for a law enforcement group. That too had failed, and she was returned again to the concentration camp.

It only took a few minutes to discover that, like Twelve, Samantha had retained her free-roaming spirit. Unlike him, however, she was forceful in expressing her resistance to having a different life. She was relatively easy to halter, but if she didn't want to travel in a certain direction or became frightened by something she didn't understand, Samantha would become indomitable. Although she was only three when she was captured, the director thought it was likely she had been a lead mare.

I adopted her that same day, then hurried back to Los Angeles to get ready for what I couldn't wait to happen.

TOPANGA

My residence was north of L.A. in a long-established village high on the inland side of the coastal mountains overlooking the Pacific Ocean. The weather there is extraordinarily serene, the vegetation overwhelmingly beautiful, and crime practically nonexistent among the wildly diverse residents, who range from musicians to immigrant workers, pot dealers, and multimillionaire film directors.

In addition to a few restaurants, gift shops, a gas station, and a dry-cleaning establishment, the little town of Topanga had a huge stable located off the main road, with barn stalls, turnouts, several riding arenas, and even a space for dressage. There was a pathway leading up to the rugged coastal mountain, and several acres on one side had been fenced to hold a dozen or more horses, two of which belonged to me.

One was an Arabian from California who had been declared untrainable and was constantly referred to as a "project," so I named him Project. He was instrumental in bringing my body back from a first bout with cancer by carrying me bareback every other day for miles and miles over the mountains above the sea.

The other horse's name was Reno. He was a strong, cooperative gelding from the state of South Dakota. If Academy Awards were given to animals, Reno would easily have won Best Supporting Actor for *Dances with Wolves*: he was the horse ridden by the character Lieutenant John Dunbar as well as a vicious Pawnee in three striking sequences in the film.

Weeks before, I had approached the tall and powerful woman who owned and managed the expansive stable about bringing in a new horse. Around her customers—most of whom were wealthy—she acted like a somewhat dictatorial but fair football coach. However, when I asked her if I could fence

Working with Twelve, Nevada, 1991

off two more acres higher on the path to the mountains for a wild horse from Nevada, she had been captivated by the idea enough to say:

"All right . . . as long as you pay for it."

The space for Twelve had been completed when I made my last return from Palomino. Now I asked if two horses rather than one could reside in the new setting, and the owner once again said,

"All right . . . but you'll have to pay rent for two."

The director and his sweet, supportive wife offered to transport Twelve and Samantha to their new home. When I insisted that they should be paid, they refused; I did manage to persuade them to accept a few days in a comfortable hotel along the beach.

With the horses' arrival less than a week away, I began to tremble. The anticipation was greater than any Christmas Eve I had experienced as a child. Impatience, worry, and longing swirled around my heart like a tropical storm.

The next day, as I went by the horse school with its hundreds of students, the swirling halted for a few moments: as I passed through the classrooms and athletic fields, I was stopped by one of the workers, who told me with a touch of anxiety that the owner needed to see me as soon as possible.

Her office was a tack room, and she was behind a desk with a cigarette in one hand, a bottle of beer in the other. Leaning forward in her chair, she took my hand and shook it. She pointed for me to sit down.

Something was up, and I knew it would come out quick—she wasn't a mincer of words. Her only preparation was two or three hurried taps to put out her cig.

19

BELOW:
Twelve, Nevada, 1991

"I'm not sure about these horses you're bringing. I'm not sure we can take 'em now."

Though stunned, I managed to speak. "What's the problem?"

"Well, a lot of people are getting worried . . . they're concerned about their horses, they . . . well . . . they're worried about disease."

In disbelief, I listened as she went on.

"They've got to vaccinate . . . uh . . . not sure what to vaccinate for . . . they . . . uh . . . they don't know what to do but leave. I don't want 'em to do that. I . . ."

With a sudden short drop of her lower lip, she stopped talking. She was staring at me as I worked to stifle laughter. I succeeded, but my face remained lit up with glee.

"I'm sorry," I managed to say, "I don't mean to put you down or anything . . . it's just that it's backwards. If you compare disease in domestic horses to disease in wild horses . . . wild horses don't have any."

Her eyes widened.

I continued. "Right now they're in Nevada being stuck over and over with needles full of stuff that will protect *them.*"

With a half-smile she shook her high-haired head in a manner that suggested embarrassment.

"You don't have to believe me . . . call anybody you want, they'll tell you the same thing."

Looking at me, she nodded.

"When are they coming?"

"Friday."

I stood up and started to turn away.

"You want a beer?" she asked gruffly.

ABOVE:
Twelve arriving in California, 1991

The sun was starting down when Samantha and Twelve backed out of the trailer in Topanga. Dozens of people were watching as they came out, and television cameras were pointed at them. Both horses were curious about their new location. I walked them to the acreage, took them in, turned them loose, and then stood and watched. I was gratified beyond anything I could have conceived.

They would spend less than half a year in Topanga, but for Twelve and Samantha the time was comfortable. The weather was always good, and they were far removed from the overcrowded conditions of the stable. People frequently hiked the easy quarter mile up the hill to observe these wild horses, the likes of which they had never seen before. For Twelve and Samantha, the brief stay was a peaceful transition from the concentration camp to their soon-to-be-permanent home.

In the years to come, I recorded our experiences together on paper from time to time; excerpts from these journals are scattered throughout this memorial. The first was written in Topanga.

1991

In more than twenty years as a horse, Twelve had never experienced a carrot. He shied from the first one I offered. I kept trying and eventually was able to slip a piece through his lips. He opened his mouth and let the unknown food fall to the ground.

The next time I tried he began to chew and has been chewing ever since. He has not missed his twice-a-day ration since he arrived at Wolf House [my ranch in Arizona].

When it's time for food, Twelve stays step for step with whoever delivers it. His eyes are forward, not on the bran or hay but on the fingers that carry the wonderful orange stick.

I not only wanted to just spend time with horse number 1202, but I also wanted to observe his reactions to things he had never before encountered.

20

In the several months that Twelve spent in California at a high-class riding stable, I would often take him for walks. I thought it might interest him to view the activities and equipment at a modern horse operation. We explored the dressage pit, the barns, the haylofts, tack rooms, and jumping arenas. Twelve responded to everything with his usual dignified curiosity.

It was a busy place, and I was often worried about something frightening him. If Twelve wanted to escape, he would do so—it would be impossible to stop him.

But the Mexican men on their tractors, the young girls twittering like birds, the electric clippers, and the horses being sprayed in wash racks did not affect him. Sometimes he would stop and stand to watch something of interest, and that was all.

He was least interested in the horses themselves. To him, I believe, a domestic horse is an inept prisoner, neither threatening nor challenging. From the beginning he has ignored domesticated horses, avoiding them when they come near.

It was on one of these walks that Twelve unwittingly revealed a part of his past to me. We paused at a riding arena because a class was in progress. Young girls were circling the arena on their horses as the pestering voice of an instructor guided them through a public address system.

As we watched, Twelve seemed more interested in what the horses were doing than in the horses themselves. His attention wandered a little as the students first walked, then obeyed a command for the horses to trot. For most of the bored school horses, the trot was more like a plod, but when they picked up the pace I could feel Twelve stiffen next to me.

The students were ordered to walk, and Twelve relaxed again. When the command to canter was given, he hurled himself to one side and wheeled into a fixed position. I tried to calm him with words and reached out to touch his neck, but he moved away without looking at my hand. Every muscle in his body had gone rigid as steel, and his eyes never wavered from a focus he held at the rear of the loping horses.

He stood like that for several moments, as if expecting something to appear. Slightly confused, he glanced at the galloping horses, then at the spot behind them. After a few more moments, he gradually relaxed again, then sighed as if bored with the whole thing.

I couldn't figure out what had startled him until we were halfway back to his and Samantha's big corral on the hill. Nothing I could see could have caused his alarm; it didn't make sense. But suddenly I realized that it made perfect sense: What we could not see was what had tripped a siren in Twelve's brain. He could not see what had caused the horses in the arena to run, so he had reacted as a defender of the herd. He had turned to make himself ready for the unseen predator.

his eyes never wavered from a focus he held at the rear of the loping horses

21

Although Topanga was a peaceful, beautiful place, leaving it was inevitable. I had lived everywhere in Los Angeles—surviving mostly hand to mouth—for a dozen years, but the success of *Dances with Wolves* and the earnings it produced gave me an opportunity to make a major change.

I purchased a magnificent thirty-six-acre ranch at the base of a stunning line of mountains Southern Arizonans call Sky Islands. Isolated in a wilderness filled with everything from mice to mountain lions, it provided long-wished-for sanctuary for a single man and his animal family. There was a large, well-built barn with multiple stalls, turnouts, a large arena, and protected natural vistas that could not be altered. The ranch, named Wolf House in honor of Jack London, had property lines set against an eighty-thousand-acre national park.

This major move, which of course involved Twelve and Samantha, began early in 1992.

ARIZONA

Because I had to go get the ranch ready, I left my brother Jim in Topanga to oversee the loading and transport of the four horses, Reno, Project, Samantha, and Twelve. The company he hired to move them was highly professional; they carried horses around the country in haulers, not in trailers. The haulers provided separate stalls with food, water, and ample space. They were so high off the ground, however, that loading had to be done with a walled ramp.

The day of the horses' scheduled departure, I stayed close to the phone waiting for a call—and one came in late morning. My brother immediately informed me that things were going well: Reno, Project, and Samantha were already inside the hauler.

"What about Twelve?" I asked.

"Oh, they're having a little trouble getting him on. He doesn't want to go up the ramp."

"Is he jumping around or anything?"

"No, he just refuses to go up."

"What are they going to do?"

"All they told me was that they've been in business sixteen years, and in sixteen years they've never had a horse they couldn't load."

The comment was encouraging, but after I hung up worry settled in and didn't leave until the phone rang again a couple of hours later.

"Well," my brother said, sounding somewhat harried, "make reservations for three."

"They couldn't get him on?"

"Nope."

A week later, Twelve was successfully loaded into a regular horse trailer, and he headed east to Arizona.

BELOW:
Twelve and Samantha playing, 1992

For Twelve the unsettling months of the adoption, travel, temporary residence in California, and then additional travel across the southwestern desert to southern Arizona finally came to a close in April.

1992

The night he came to Arizona was a sleepless one for me. The people I had hired to trailer him from California called about four o'clock in the morning, and I hurried down to the road in front of the gatehouse to meet them.

It was a black night, and I called into the stock trailer because I could not see him. It was foolish to call—I have never heard him vocalize to another horse; his language comes entirely from his body movement. I thought I could sense his presence inside, but not being able to see made me edgy after I'd waited so long. The transporter followed me to where a dirt road cutoff to the barn. In the darkness before the dawn, they opened a side door at the front of the long trailer, and I looked inside.

Soft, golden light from the cab was filtering through the back window. It floated around his body. He stood quietly on the wooden floor, all alone in the big trailer, like some beautiful monster from another world. His arrival seemed like a miracle.

Twelve and Samantha, who were initially kept separate from the domestic horses, shared a large stall and a half-acre turnout. A gate could be opened that would allow access to a big arena. When I began to let them out, what happened was so remarkable that I began to carry a camera in order to capture it.

1993

Samantha had been adopted as a companion for Twelve, and she was a perfect choice. Though she has become quite tame, the wild blood will always be a part of her, and that blood is Twelve's only connection with his free past.

When they first came to Arizona, I would keep them confined each night and turn them out to play each morning in the big arena. They never failed to put on a magnificent show. They took turns chasing each other around the open ground. When cornered, Twelve would rear, sometimes walking on his hind legs as he pawed the air around Samantha's head. She too would rise to meet him, and amazingly, they never so much as nicked each other with their sharp, heavy hooves.

The playful battles would last a half hour or more. Twelve would provoke Samantha, nudging her neck with his powerful head or nipping at her shoulder with his teeth. Then, to his delight, Samantha would chase him. Twelve would run to one corner or another of the arena where Samantha would try to cut off his escape routes. The old stallion's moves were as deft and expert as any great athlete's. Boxed in,

he would twist or turn or dive out of her reach. *If these moves failed, he would rise as only Twelve could, and Samantha had no choice but to let him escape. After a round of the spirited game they would break for a minute or two before Twelve provoked her again, starting another cycle of breathtaking play.*

Such dramatic displays are routine in the free life of wild horses. It not only gives them great pleasure, but it also keeps them in top shape and serves as instruction for younger members of their families.

In the second year after their arrival in Arizona, this play gradually petered out and then stopped altogether. Sadly for me, they won't be playing again: after so much time in captivity it is no longer necessary, and they both know it. Samantha no longer needs Twelve as she once did. She has formed a leading relationship with the domestic horses, too.

The old stallion has accepted retirement, and I don't think he misses all the rearing and whirling of those winter mornings. But he has no interest of any kind in the other horses either, and while he may accept his fate, he has not changed. He is a prisoner of his past, of wild blood.

Despite this, the bond between him and Samantha is still strong and always will be. There are flashes of it from time to time.

All of the horses spend their days together but are isolated while they eat so that they may enjoy their dinner without distractions. In the early evening we go down to turn them out, and at sunset not long ago, while the others were still busy with their hay, Twelve made a purposeful walk to Samantha's pen where he stood in wistful silence at her open gate, waiting respectfully for her to come out. When Samantha saw him standing there, she trotted happily to meet him and they immediately began to groom each other, nibbling along each other's necks in the classic affectionate style of wild horses.

Little Boy emerged from his stall, and seeing Twelve and Samantha together, decided to break them up. But the moment was precious to Sam, and she would tolerate no interruption. Pinning her ears, she showed Little Boy her rear, and in a few moments she had driven him off. Then she and Twelve continued their ritual of love and devotion, stopping only when they were satisfied it had been completed.

Despite the joy Twelve and Samantha shared in the arena, a pair of events early on made it clear that there was more on Twelve's mind than the relative comfort of his new confinement.

1992

In his early months in Arizona, he escaped twice through gates left open. Each time he went straight to the business of trying to find out how to get off the ranch; each time he tried to reach the mountains. Fortunately, a series of gates leading to the national park were shut both times, and he was brought back. It often crossed my mind that if Twelve reached the mountains he would be lost to us forever, and that being lost

25

ABOVE:
Twelve and Samantha playing, 1992

LEFT:
Twelve awaiting transport, Nevada, 1991

forever might not be so bad—let the old stallion go into the mountains and spend his last days in freedom.

1992

The creeks were still running well into April and May the year Twelve came to Arizona. I took him for walks frequently, and one day I decided to see how he would react to the biggest creek in the area, which was about a mile away. We set out on a warm but not blistering-hot morning. There was a light cooling breeze, the kind that makes for a perfect day.

We walked along a road he had not been down before, and as usual he showed a mild, alert curiosity about man-made things. In the desert, he strolled without a care. When we crested a hill he would stop and take a sighting, as if he was mapping the area. Then he would sigh before shoving off, or just turn his head and start to walk.

Twelve is not the kind of being that can be led—rather, he is guided.

As we neared the creek he perked up, and by the time we turned off the road and navigated through the mesquite, he was very alert. When we got to the stream his desire could have been read by anyone: he wanted to get in the water.

He waded right in, walking up and down as I held the lead line. He sniffed the surface several times, but that was not enough. I had the feeling that he wanted to explore this water that surely reminded him of his wild life, so I slipped off my boots and socks, rolled my Levi's to my knees, and followed him in.

The water was only a foot or two deep, and we plowed up and down for a few minutes. Then we went upstream and found a deeper pool at a bend in the stream. Twelve wanted to wade in immediately, but I wanted to go with him, and after tugging persistently at the line, he followed me to shore and waited impatiently as I struggled out of my clothes (I left on my broad-brimmed hat but nothing else).

We returned to the pool, and Twelve started to paw at the water with a foreleg, a sure sign that he was going down. He dropped to his knees and tumbled to one side, rolling joyfully in the cool water. I found myself sitting down with him, and though the water was chilly, I hardly noticed. We were together in the stream. He rolled completely over and bathed his other side while I sat still, holding the line limply in my hand. To be with this great horse in such an intimate way lifted my spirits as few events can. He rolled in the water with the joy of ancient reunion, and as I squatted next to him I could only think of the rare privilege that had somehow been granted me.

Before my second bout with cancer, I devoted the majority of my time to bringing public attention to the devastation being visited on wild horses. As a result I was often away from home, and I often returned to that same hotel in Reno.

ABOVE:
Twelve in Arizona, free at last, 1995

26

From a gilded rookery on the twenty-second floor of a casino hotel, I can clearly see the bare hills to the east. Not far beyond this unbroken line lies his horse range and the site of his capture.

This pile of human rubble I am sitting on top of is connected to the ruination of his freedom. The materials from which the hotel was constructed are connected to the voracious appetites of the gamblers on the floors below and their craving for fancy food, drinks, and clothes. It's even connected to the parade of classic cars and the thousands lined up to watch them creep past underneath my window. All these things have hastened the extinction of free lives. It is true freedom, freedom that has been pushed aside to make room for the avarice that drives the human race toward what will be a long fall.

The city of Reno is a magnet for self-indulgence that cannot be satisfied, and I am sitting on top of the swirly, maggot-ridden magnet.

Back in Arizona he is standing in his stall, probably enjoying his never-changing dinner. Perhaps he is scratching his bottom in the crook of the dead mesquite tree. Maybe he is standing alone in the arena, smelling rain coming up from Mexico. Whatever he may be doing at this moment, it is of no harm to anyone or anything. He has never performed a destructive act in his life. Lying or cheating for personal gain is not part of his being, nor is the accumulation of wealth for its own sake. The only system he is part of is that of the Creator.

It's a long climb to New Pass Summit and a welcome one after covering so many empty, flat miles. From a distance the Desatoya Mountains look like a fortress, and they were for Twelve. It's likely he was born somewhere in these mountains. He roamed them for more than twenty years before being captured on March 12, 1990.

The capture site was listed as New Pass Summit, but as I labored up the grade it was hard to imagine anyone catching him in these tough, jagged mountains. However, as I crested the grade, it became obvious. The land flattened out and stretched itself into a wide valley of sagebrush cut by the inevitable ranch roads, and I knew that it was here they had finally caught him.

I wanted to stop, to walk the earth he had walked, to smell the same air and view the same sights. But the horrible history of this place, the thought of horses cleaned out as they have been in so many other places, drove me on.

As I crossed over the summit, I considered the challenges he faced in so many years of roaming free in a hostile land: defending himself—against helicopters, trucks, and men carrying guns—with a savvy head, four strong legs, and nothing else.

But he and hundreds of thousands like him are gone now from this beautiful land, and for that

he has never performed a destructive act in his life

27

reason alone I could not stop as I traveled over four hundred miles of Nevada roads. Something evil is still afoot in this land, and it has left its imprint everywhere. In all those miles of open, free country, the mark of evil is present in what is absent. The wild horses are missing from the land.

Little Boy was a two-year-old I received as a wedding gift. For years we rode together over mountains and plains. When Twelve would no longer accept being associated with domestic horses, Samantha and Little Boy became a couple.

1993

As far as we know Twelve no longer thinks of escape. Now we occasionally let him out on his own. Usually he spends a few minutes with his nose in the grass. Then he comes back to see if there's some alfalfa lying on the barn floor for him to nibble.

Every once in a while he will wander up a neighbor's driveway to high ground. There he can watch mile after mile of open landscape. He comes back down like an elderly gentleman who has lapsed into a dream of his past.

He has never forgotten his responsibilities as a stallion. When a wildfire burned within view of the barn, he stood in a high paddock, closest to the fire, viewing it intensely. Samantha stood on the other end of the arena near the gate, ready to lead. The domestic horses stood between them, not quite comprehending what the burning land meant.

Several days a week he receives Samantha in a separate stall we call "Twelve's penthouse." It makes his day complete to have her with him. He hovers around her but never in a suffocating way. He pays her every attention while respecting her every shift of mood.

They are so tame now that I can stand next to them as they go through the thorough, time-consuming ritual of grooming. It is as intimate as watching a man and woman bathing in the same tub, yet they let me watch, and the honor of it makes me wonder if there is anything else I can do to make them happy.

I know that Twelve is happy. He is so old now that I truly believe he enjoys the rich alfalfa he gets twice a day. I think he loves getting a drink of cool water whenever he wants it. He is groomed and walked each day and has Samantha to himself for a few hours. He eats his meals without harassment and has his bedding changed when needed.

At night all the horses are reunited after dinner. Samantha and Reno and Little Boy are usually busy browsing in the stray bits of hay that were dropped during their foraging. This presents Twelve an opportunity to have a few moments of solitary pleasure. He shuffles down to Samantha's paddock for a rendezvous with the dead mesquite tree standing there. Twelve has a good feeling about the tree, and he

28

he has never forgotten his responsibilities as a stallion

treats it well, never breaking branches as he massages himself against its limbs. He's found a place, a certain crook that will accommodate his small round bottom. He backs in and sways from side to side like a rumba dancer.

Invariably, the other horses will finish their browsing and reappear, but by that time Twelve will be finished. He seems to know exactly how much time he has and how to use it.

He is full of surprises, but after reflection each wonder of 1202 seems like it could have been predicted. He never utters a word, but his unheard language is a sophisticated gem. He is never too weak and never too strong. His vigilance is automatic. He is gentle at every opportunity. He never has to worry. Twelve knows himself, and at his core is the contentment reserved for only the highest beings of this world.

1995

When I am far away from him, normal anxieties about his health and well-being never last long. They are overwhelmed in the same way a great wave covers everything, in the way lava engulfs all in its path, in the same way a great wind sweeps all from its route. Whenever I am gone, I know that he cannot die. His passing as a living thing of the earth will be noticed only by me and a few others, but his being will live forever. He is all I know of eternity. That he breathes or not somehow makes little difference when I am away. When I am away I see him as indestructible as the earth itself. He is forever. I don't worry about him at all.

Quanah was a medium-sized bay that I purchased from a rental stable for five hundred dollars in the late 1980s. He was marvelous to ride, especially bareback. I discovered that he had originally been a wild horse captured in Idaho. Immediately after he died, something happened that I had to record.

1995

On the day that Quanah was put out of his misery, he could barely walk. After ten minutes of encouragement, the old man who had given so much pleasure to so many was only able to make it from his pen into the arena—each step had taken great courage, but he could move no more. The doctor injected him with a powerful painkiller, and in a few minutes my old friend was walking. I led him down the road to the spot where the vet and his assistant were waiting for us, out of sight of the other horses.

The other horses knew something final was happening. How they knew is a mystery, in the same way that dogs know a trip is inevitable before the first suitcase is opened for packing. Samantha and Reno and Little Boy were all nervous, and Twelve stood in the middle of the arena, watching every movement and listening to every sound with perfect concentration.

After Quanah had died and the vet and his helper had gone, I sat down on the ground just outside

ABOVE:
Twelve and Samantha at Wolf House, Arizona, 1994

BELOW:
Twelve and Samantha, Arizona, 2001

Samantha's stall in a stupor of grief. As I sat tearful and cross-legged on the dirt, I was surprised to see Twelve walking up to me, his muzzle so low that his eyes were almost level with mine. He moved his nose around my hands. I thought he was looking for something to eat, so I told him I didn't have anything. Preoccupied with the passing of Quanah, I let my thoughts drift off. The next thing I heard was my wife's voice, remarking on Twelve.

"What?" I said.

"Look at him."

Twelve was still standing in front of me, his head almost in my lap.

"He's consoling you," she said.

She was right.

1996

He used to rear all the time. He would rear against the blacksmith who tried to trim his hooves. He reared against the vet who tried to examine him. In play he reared constantly over Samantha.

Now he rears only rarely, but he managed to get into the air when I tried to rub some salve on a patch of dry skin under his armpit.

As he went up I was reminded that in all the times I have seen him rise on his hind legs, he has never shown intent to harm. It has always been a display and nothing more, a demonstration of his power. He knows he is a captive, and I believe he accepts it, but when I see this power I cannot imagine that anything could defeat him.

ABOVE:
Michael and Twelve, 1991

RIGHT:
Twelve's last day in Nevada, 1991

Throughout the fourteen years we spent together, any discernable feelings Twelve might have had of connection with me, his adopter, were few and far between. The lack of a bond between us had no effect on me emotionally, but when there *were* signs of closeness, I was compelled to write it down.

1997

Most often Twelve's attitude is standoffish, but there are times when his attitude is dramatically different. When I've been away from him for more than a day or two, he, unlike any horse I have known, seems genuinely pleased at my return. After being gone for nine days I opened the stall door this afternoon and he stood perfectly still as I worked my finger around his sensitive eyes. Usually he pulls his head to one side or another, and almost always I will have to halter him to get down to business. But this afternoon he just stood. In fact, he lifted his head up and held it like a good patient in the examining room. He'd left some of his dinner on the floor, and when I offered him some of the discarded hay he eventually took a bite. Twelve wasn't interested, but he chewed a mouthful anyway.

It was unusual. His behavior all around was characteristically uncooperative. I can only conclude that he was happy to see me and expressed it. Every encounter with him, no matter whether it is momentous or trivial, is shaded with a quality of wonder.

1998

Twelve loves water, but not from a hose. When I turn on the spigot to soak a sponge for him, he gives the lead line a twist with his great neck, pulling me off my feet.

I always hope he will accept the hose, but he never does. When he pulls away, I go to him; I stroke his muzzle and talk in reassuring tones. In a few moments he consents to come forward again, close enough for me to reach out with a free hand and turn off the water.

1999

The summer sun in Arizona is monstrous. It burns with the intensity of flame, pounding on every living thing from sunup to sundown. The nights provide barely enough renewal to get through the next smoldering day.

The horses are listless in the heat, their days spent in a torpor as they move from shade to sun and back to shade with no escape from the swarms of insects that thrive in the daily inferno.

Twelve bears it with his usual regal manner. His black coat absorbs the fiery heat as a sponge does water. His large wet eyes are feeding stations for the relentless gnats and flies, and at the end of each brutal day they are swollen and running.

Through each day and night he stands impervious, his ears still cocked at every nuance of sound, his eyes focused and cool, the great head and neck never hanging in sorrow. Were he to break a leg, his demeanor would be the same. And if he had ever made it to the slaughterhouse floor, the butchers would have marveled at how many shots it took to kill him.

2004

He stands alone in the last stall of the barn, like a king without a country. When they sliced off his manhood, they threw a whole way of life into the garbage. No king could ever suffer a greater calamity than he has suffered, yet his majesty remains until the last day of his life. He stands unconfused; his ears are cocked forward, his muscles poised for action. He is the true king, not because of clever marriages or other worldly intrigues or men's manipulations. He rose with the surety of an angel's flight, infused with wisdom and strength. He is the greatest of stallions, simply superior to all.

Long live the king.

ABOVE:
Twelve and Samantha playing, 1992

32

THE END

Life is death.

Death is life.

The permanent connection between life and death is resisted, ignored, or disbelieved by a vast majority of humanity. Twelve understood the connection and fully accepted the inevitability of leaving earth.

In 2003 he was around thirty-five years old and steadily deteriorating physically. Injuries he had once overcome were making themselves known again, making movement more and more difficult. His spirit was still in place, but it was obvious that it was dimming in the same way light fades at the end of each day.

In the summer, he stopped eating for the first time.

Before his longtime veterinarian was able to make it out to the ranch, Twelve did something he had not done for a decade: he left the ranch. After an intense search, we found him near a creek a mile away, and we brought him back.

The vet's examination revealed that his kidney function had dropped nearly eighty percent—any more of a drop would insure death. Injected with medication, the kidneys regained some function, and he began to eat again. While I was relieved, I doubt that it mattered to Twelve. His escape had been made for a reason. He had accepted the arrival of death, and his departure from the people and animals he had lived with for more than a decade was designed to let death come.

Though his eyes were fading and his legs were increasingly unable to carry his body, he continued to eat for several years. At the end of the summer in 2005, however, his kidneys once again began to collapse, and for the second time he lost the ability to eat. The diagnosis and treatment were the same as before, but this time the medication had little effect, and he refused to take the pills he had been assigned.

I found myself emotionally sandwiched between life and death. Although I wanted to let him pass away naturally, it was equally excruciating to see the incessant suffering he was enduring.

A week or two later, I made an observation that provoked overpowering depression. One night, as I drove up the dirt road to the house, I passed a corner where miles of fence came together (years before, several acres around the barn had been fenced to keep the horses from intruding on the property of other ranch owners). He was there, standing perfectly still, his eyes focused on the outside. It was the first time I had ever seen him standing with hope—hope that somehow the fence would open.

Wanting to support his desire to be free but not being able to make it happen was devastating. Letting him out could easily subject him to unwanted intervention from my neighbors—even leading

he was there, standing perfectly still, his eyes focused on the outside

33

him up to the mountains and letting him go could not guarantee that his life would end in solace.

Hoping that death would be able to take him down on its own, I waited. He had stopped drinking as well as eating, his body had thinned to bone, his brain had dropped to a lack of awareness, but death was still unable to take him to the ground.

On September 7, 2005, Twelve was injected with death by a doctor. It would have been far better if his spirit could have departed as he ran free to his own death site. In the end, however, there was no choice.

He was buried in a large grave covered with a high mound a hundred yards from the barn he had lived in for fourteen years. Although his age could not be proven, it was somewhere in the vicinity of forty years.

A body is not a spirit, but I wanted his physical remains to be treated with reverence—the incredible being named Twelve had lived inside it. I have visited his grave nearly every day since he died, driven not so much by grief as a sense of honor.

The spirit that inspired every person and animal who experienced it is no longer active, but is not altogether gone. Twelve sired scores of descendants, and his spirit still lives on in any who have survived the incessant slaughter of wild horses over the last several decades.

The same spirit has been installed in this human heart, and it will remain there as long as my heart beats.

his spirit still lives on in any who have survived the incessant slaughter

RIGHT:
Twelve at rest forever, Arizona, 2005

ABOVE:
Michael at gravesite, Arizona, 2005

PREVIOUS BOOKS BY MICHAEL BLAKE

Fiction:
Dances with Wolves
Airman Mortensen
Marching to Valhalla
The Holy Road

Nonfiction:
Like a Running Dog
Indian Yell